We all have the right to life.

Nobody has the right to hurt or torture us.

We all want a good life, to have fun, to be safe and happy and fulfilled.

For this to happen we need to look after each other. Here in the United Kingdom there are sixteen different freedoms that help look after us. They are truly wonderful, precious things.

I've drawn some pictures for you. Each of them shows one of our freedoms. I hope you like them.

These freedoms were created to protect every one of us, forever. They are part of something called THE HUMAN RIGHTS ACT.

We need to stand up for these freedoms and look after them just as they look after us.

Chris Riddell.

UK CHILDREN'S LAUREATE

Nobody has the right to make us a slave - We cannot make anyone else a slave or force them to work for us.

No one has the right to lock us up without a good reason. They have to tell us that reason and let us say why we should be set free.

If we are put on trial we must be treated fairly. Nobody can blame us for doing something bad until it is proved. The people who try us must not let anyone else tell them what to do.

You can't be punished for doing something wrong if there was no law against it when you did it.

FAMILY

We have the right to live with our family and live our lives in the way we choose. The government shouldn't spy on us.

We all have the right to think or believe in whatever we like, to have a religion and to show it.

THOUGHT

We all have the right to the information we need to make up our own minds. We have the right to say what we think and share ideas with other people.

We all have the right to spend time with other people and get together to look after each other.

Every grown-up has the right to marry and have a family if they want to.

We all have the same rights.
No-one can take them away
or give us different ones because
of who we are, or because we
are different from them.

Everybody has the right to own and share things. Nobody should take our things away without a good reason.

KNOWLEDGE

We all have the right
to learn.

We all have the right to take part in running our country. Every grown-up should be allowed to say who they want to be their leader.

No one is allowed to kill us, even if we did something very bad.

## Why this little book is important

The pictures in this beautiful book are about human rights. These are special rules that belong to all of us, and look after us all. We may not have our own lion to guard our freedom, or a Pegasus to wrap its wings around us, but here in the UK we do have a special law called the Human Rights Act. It looks after all of us, children and grown-ups, just because we are human.

The Human Rights Act helps to keeps us safe. Every day.

We have simplified the words of the Human Rights Act in this little book. You can find out more and see the full list at **amnesty.org.uk/humanrightsact**

# More lovely books from Amnesty

With illustrations by award-winning artists from all over the world,
published for Amnesty by Frances Lincoln Children's Books.

**We Are All Born Free:**
The Universal Declaration of Human Rights in pictures

*Outstanding International Book* – US Board on Books for Young People

*A copy in every classroom would be a good start, but ideally every child
should start life with one of their own* – Telegraph

Winner, English Association Special Award, Best Children's Illustrated
Books 2008

**Dreams of Freedom:** in words and pictures

*A priceless gem* – Booktrust

You can see more at **amnesty.org.uk/books** and buy through all good
bookshops and at **amnestyshop.org.uk**

I WANT TO DRAW
EVERYDAY AS CHILDREN'S
LAUREATE AND
PROMOTE DRAWING
FOR ALL

← THE
LAUREATE
LOG

ILLUSTRATED BY CHRIS RIDDELL